# Contents

# Gymnastics

▲
Judges watch a gymnast as he competes on the vault during the 2008 European Men's Artistic Gymnastics Championships which were held in Switzerland.

Gymnastics is the name for a group of sports for boys and girls that tests their balance, strength and flexibility. People were performing gymnastics more than 3,000 years ago, which makes it one of the oldest sports in the world.

Modern gymnastics has three main strands: trampolining, artistic gymnastics and rhythmic gymnastics. In artistic gymnastics athletes perform moves on pieces of equipment called apparatus (see panel on page 7).

Rhythmic gymnastics is a competition event that is mostly performed by girls. It takes place on a large mat on the floor. Gymnasts complete attractive, flowing routines set to music. They perform with certain objects such as a ball, a ribbon or a large hoop.

# Aberdeenshire
## COUNCIL

Aberdeenshire Library and Information Service
www.aberdeenshire.gov.uk/libraries
Renewals Hotline 01224 661511

G                                              CS

ALIS

3018006

Published in 2010 by Evans Publishing Ltd,
2A Portman Mansions,
Chiltern St, London WIU 6NR

Editor: Nicola Edwards
Designer: D.R. Ink
All photographs by Wishlist except for page 6 FABRICE COFFRINI/AFP/Getty Images; page 10 Shaun Botterill/Getty Images; page 11 KAZUHIRO NOGI/Getty Images; page 25 AFP/Getty Images; page 26 Clive Brunskill/Getty Images, page 27 AFP/Getty Images

British Library Cataloguing in Publication Data

Gifford, Clive.

Gymnastics. -- (Tell me about sport)
1. Gymnastics--Juvenile literature.
I. Title II. Series
796.4'4-dc22
ISBN-13: 9780237541538

Printed in China.

The author and publisher would like to thank Corey Newton, Zoe Jones, Lottie Brown, Drew Lenihan-Orwa, Georgia Clarke, Teya Agnese and Ryan Wantajja, Coach Mel Wade and Wade Gymnastics Club for their help with the photographs for this book.

## Artistic gymnastics apparatus

**Male gymnasts**
Pommel horse, high bar, vault, rings, floor routine, parallel bars.

**Female gymnasts**
Floor routine, vault, uneven (or asymmetrical) bars, balance beam

▶ This gymnast is performing a forward somersault. She springs up and makes a complete turn in the air before landing on her feet.

Whatever type of gymnastics you decide to take part in, you can be certain that you will improve your agility and fitness when you take up the sport. Gymnastics is hard work but it is a real thrill to perfect an exciting new move. Most schools teach some gymnastics and many also run after school sessions for those interested in learning the sport. Gym classes are often held at local clubs and at leisure centres.

▼ These gymnasts are practising some of the body positions used in gymnastics. Learning positions and movements such as cartwheels and somersaults at a gym class can be great fun.

# Gym kit and clothing

You need very little special equipment or clothing to take up gymnastics. At the very start, you can just wear shorts and a t-shirt. As you get more into the sport, you may prefer to wear the proper clothing: a leotard with sleeves for girls and a sleeveless leotard and shorts for boys for most events.

▼ Gymnasts finish their routines with their feet together, their chests forwards with their backs straight and their arms poised.

Before training or performing you must remove all jewellery, and if you have long hair you should tie it up. Gymnastics is usually performed barefoot but some gymnasts wear gym shoes which are similar to ballet shoes. Gymnasts may wear socks when they are performing on some pieces of apparatus, such as the bars and rings.

Apart from a tracksuit to keep you warm and a water bottle to drink from, you will find everything else you need at your gym club. This includes the apparatus you will perform on as well as the training equipment.

Your coach or teacher will take you through all the safety rules in your gym before you begin to train. He or she will also teach you a series of exercises and stretches for you to perform at the start of each class. These will help to warm up your body and loosen your muscles and joints. You need to be really flexible to perform gymnastics. This is the ability to bend all of your body parts well.

▶

This gymnast is wearing long gymnastic trousers called Sokol pants. He also wears handguards which help improve grip and can stop blisters forming. Gymnasts wear handguards when they perform on apparatus such as the rings and bars.

▼ Many gymnasts put powdered chalk on their feet and hands to improve their grip and stop them slipping. Here, a gymnast dips his hands in a chalk box. He then rubs them together to make sure his fingers and palms are covered.

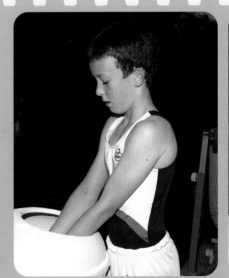

# Gymnastics stars

Gymnasts work long and hard with their coaches in order to be able to perform at their peak in major competitions such as world championships and the Olympics. Russia, Eastern Europe, China, Japan and the United States have produced most of the world's top gymnasts.

The most talented gymnasts often compete in a number of the individual apparatus events at a competition. There is also a combined event called the all-around in which gymnasts perform on four pieces of apparatus in the women's event and six in the men's.

▼

Britain's Daniel Keatings performs on the parallel bars on his way to winning the silver medal in the men's individual all-around final of the 2009 Artistic Gymnastics World Championships.

## In and out of competition

Top gymnasts used to be as young as 11 or 12. But in 1997, the International Gymnastics Federation decided that gymnasts had to be 16 or older to compete in major championships.

In 2003 Beth Tweddle became the first British gymnast to win a medal at the World Championships.

In 2008, 17 US gymnasts went on a nationwide tour performing with live music stars around 34 cities in North America.

Some gymnasts, such as Olga Korbut, Nadia Comaneci and Shannon Miller, become famous as a result of their performances. When American gymnast Shawn Johnson won a gold medal at the 2008 Olympics in Beijing, she became a major celebrity in the United States, appearing in adverts and winning a reality TV dancing show.

Because elite gymnasts push themselves so hard in order to be the best, they sometimes suffer injuries. These can be frustrating as they can take long periods to recover from. For example, top Russian gymnast Anna Pavlova tore two knee ligaments at the end of her beam routine during a competition in November 2008. She needed surgery and didn't compete again in a major event until more than a year later.

◀

Shawn Johnson only entered senior adult gymnastics in 2007 but the next year at the age of 16 she won an Olympic gold on the balance beam as well as three silvers in the all-around, the team competition and the floor routine.

# Basic moves

Many basic gymnastics moves are all about making attractive, accurate body shapes and changing from one shape to another. Some of the moves, such as handstands and the splits, which you first learn to do on the floor, you may later learn to use on pieces of apparatus such as the balance beam. Many shapes can be made from a standing position, on the floor and in the air via jumps and leaps.

◀ This gymnast performs a handstand, supported by another gymnast. After the gymnast has kicked up her first leg, the helper supports the hips. As the second leg rises to join the first, the standing gymnast supports the lower legs.

▼ These gymnasts are performing a straddle pike jump (left) and a tuck jump. For a good tuck jump, you bring your knees up tightly to your chest and keep your head up.

▲ This gymnast holds a bridge position. His head is between his arms which are stretched with the elbows pointing in the same direction as the head. The stomach and hips are pushed upwards. Both the hands and feet point in the same direction and are flat on the floor.

On the floor, gymnasts learn to make moves such as the dish, arch and bridge, which help to improve their strength and flexibility. Floor moves also include rolls, such as the backward roll, forward roll and circle roll. To perform a circle roll gymnasts hold their legs in a straddle (apart) position as they roll on their shoulder and back in a tight circle.

A balance is a body shape that is made and then held. There are many different balances including the shoulder stand balance performed on the floor and the elegant arabesque (see page 17), which is performed standing on one leg.

# Floor routines

You can combine many of the balances, rolls and other basic movements you learn to form series of moves. Once you put together several series of movements, you have the beginnings of a simple floor routine.

Floor routines are performed on a 12-metre-square mat on a springy floor. They feature leaps, jumps, hold positions such as handstands, and tumbling. This is a series of spectacular acrobatic flips, springs, cartwheels, somersaults and round-off movements.

In competitions, gymnasts take part in a compulsory routine, in which they and their competitors perform a set series of the same moves. Later, they have the

▼ This gymnast links two basic moves together. She first performs a handstand, then tips forward, tucks her legs into her chest and moves into a forward roll.

▲ This gymnast performs a backflip. She arches her back as she springs off the floor onto her hands. She shows brilliant balance and strength to land on her hands and hold a handstand position.

chance to perform their own routine. The women's routine is set to music and can be up to 90 seconds long.

The men's floor routine usually lasts between 60 and 70 seconds but is not set to music. Male gymnasts have to perform moves or positions which demonstrate their strength and control as well as performing acrobatic tumbling sequences. During the routine they must touch each corner of the mat at least once.

► This gymnast performs a cartwheel, keeping his body, arms and legs in a straight line. He places his left hand on the floor, stretches with his right, kicks up his left leg then the right and splits his legs wide as he reaches an upside-down position.

# Rhythmic gymnastics

Rhythmic gymnastics is a highly artistic side of the sport, mainly practised and performed by girls. Routines take place on a 12-metre-square mat that isn't sprung, unlike the mat used for artistic gymnastics.

The routines feature flowing, graceful moves, a little like ballet, which are set to music. Each routine features a single piece of equipment – a ball, rope, a pair of hand clubs, a large hoop or a 6m-long ribbon. In all-around competitions, gymnasts have to perform a routine with each object.

▼ This gymnast demonstrates the part of her floor routine in which she performs with a ribbon, keeping it moving throughout.

▲ The hoop is up to 90cm wide. Gymnasts can swing it around their arms, legs and body, jump through it and throw and catch it as part of a routine.

▼ This rhythmic gymnast holds a graceful arabesque position with a ball in her hand. She is balanced on one straight leg with her other leg out at 90 degrees behind her.

Each object is an important part of the routine as it is handled, balanced and moved around the gymnast's body. Young gymnasts spend a lot of time learning how to move these objects about and use them with floor balances, leaps and other moves.

A rhythmic gymnast has to follow the rules of her event. For example, in a routine with a rope, the gymnast must make at least three leaps, and whilst performing with the ribbon, a gymnast must keep it moving constantly throughout the routine. At no point can the ball be held in two hands. It must always be balanced or rolled, thrown or bounced.

Some gyms also allow boys to take part in rhythmic gymnastics which builds flexibility, balance and coordination skills. Male events have become very popular in Asia, with the very first world championships for men held in Japan in 2003.

# Vaulting

The vault is the quickest event in gymnastics. Blink and it's over! Gymnasts build up speed on their run-up. Then, they hit a device on the floor called a springboard which helps send them speeding up and forwards towards the vaulting table.

The gymnast's hands land on the table and then push off the table. The gymnast is now in the air and performs spectacular moves, such as twists, flips or somersaults, before landing on a padded mat.

Vaults are grouped into types based on the movements involved. For example, Yurchenko vaults are those that use a cartwheel to move onto the springboard.

▼ This gymnast makes her run along the runway. She builds speed before landing onto the springboard, springing up and forward. She gets her hands up ready to place them on the vaulting table.

▲ This gymnast performs a handspring vault. She pushes off the vaulting table with her hands and arms and tries to keep a straightened shape.

In competitions, a gymnast must let the judges know which type of vault they are going to perform. A vault is judged from the moment the gymnast touches the springboard. If a gymnast stops in the middle of the run-up, he or she is allowed to restart their run within 30 seconds and not lose any points.

▼ As she completes her vault, the gymnast flies off the vaulting table. She makes a perfect dismount, landing with her feet close together, her back arched and her arms and head up.

# The rings and the beam

The rings are a real test of strength for men and boys. They are suspended from a piece of apparatus so that they hang 2.75 metres above the floor. Gymnasts are helped up onto the rings and then perform a routine.

The balance beam is just 13cm wide, yet top gymnasts are able to perform jumps, springs and backflips on it. Young gymnasts learn moves on the floor on a coloured foam strip and then move up to a low beam just above the floor. Simple moves consist of sits on the beam and balance positions on one foot. Gymnasts are allowed to move backwards and forwards along the beam.

▼ Moves on the rings include backward and forward swings and a range of different hold positions such as the iron cross and the inverted crucifix. In these holds, the gymnast has to stay as still as possible.

Many gymnasts now use a springboard to spring off, perform a move in the air and then land on the narrow beam at the start of a routine which, in competitions, may last up to 90 seconds. In competition, gymnasts who fall from the beam lose 0.8 points from their score.

## Amazing achievements

In 1981, East German gymnast, Maxi Gnauck performed one of the first ever back flips off a springboard to land on the balance beam.

At the 1976 Olympics, Japan's Shun Fujimoto broke his knee cap during the men's team competition. Astonishingly, he continued to compete, performing a brilliant routine on the rings to help Japan win the gold medal.

Italian gymnast Jury Chechi won the rings competition at five World Gymnastics Championships in a row from 1993 to 1997.

 You need excellent flexibility to hold this Y-balance position on a beam.

# The bars and the pommel horse

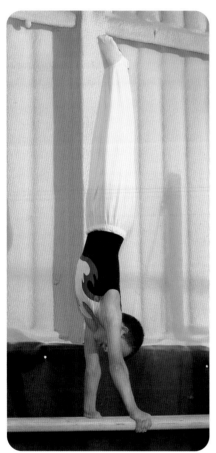

In artistic gymnastics, there are three different bars, two used by men (the parallel bars and high bar) and the uneven bars for women. The parallel bars stand two metres off the ground. Gymnasts move between and above the bars using their arms to hold certain positions including handstands, as well as swings.

The high bar stands 2.78 metres above the floor and is 2.4m long. Gymnasts perform impressive swings round using different grips of the bar as well as catch and release moves in which they let go of the bar, perform a move and grip the bar again.

▲
This gymnast holds a handstand position on the parallel bars. At the end of his routine he will perform a dismount, usually landing to the side of the bars.

▶
This gymnast is performing a catch and release move on the uneven bars.

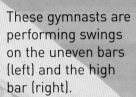

These gymnasts are performing swings on the uneven bars (left) and the high bar (right).

Performances on the uneven or asymmetrical bars are among the most spectacular in gymnastics. Female gymnasts swing on each of the bars and leap between each bar to perform catches and releases, as well as handstands.

Performing on the high and uneven bars, gymnasts aim to make a complex dismount that is both accurate and spectacular. They often build speed and momentum with swings round, launching themselves into the air to perform somersaults and twists before landing.

The pommel horse looks like an old-style vaulting horse but with two large handles on top. Gymnasts grip these handles as they perform a series of movements in a short routine that usually lasts around 25 seconds.

Working on the pommel horse, this gymnast holds a strength position, locking his arms. Keeping his legs together he swings them in a circular movement about the horse.

# Trampolining

A trampoline is a strong, tight sheet, usually made of canvas, attached with springs to a metal frame. Gymnasts build height by bouncing high above the trampoline bed and then perform a routine of moves including twists and somersaults.

Top gymnasts can reach heights of over 8 metres above the bed of the trampoline and spend nearly two seconds in the air between bounces. In most competitions, a routine is made up of ten skills or moves and gymnasts must start and finish on their feet.

▲ This gymnast performs a back somersault. Top trampolinists can manage a triple somersault in the air between each bounce.

▲ This gymnast performs a jump in the piked position with her legs straight and together and her hands close to her feet.

The trampoline first appeared as a medal sport at the Olympics in 2000. Two of the seven judges present judge the level of difficulty of the routine whilst the other five judge how well the trampolinist performs his or her routine.

Synchronised trampolining is not an Olympic sport but is an event at many other competitions. Two gymnasts perform exactly the same routine of ten skills on trampolines next to each other. They must match each other's routine with perfect timing.

▼ Judges look on as Japanese gymnasts Masaki Ito (right) and Shunsuke Nagasaki compete in a synchronized trampoling event at the World Games in 2009.

# The world of gymnastics

Gymnastics competitions vary from local and regional tournaments to national and international events such as the European Championships. Gymnastics is also a key part of many multi-sport competitions, including the Pan-American Games and the Olympics.

The World Artistic Gymnastics Championships were first held in 1903. Since 1991, they have been held every 12 months except in an Olympic year.

▼ China's Yang Wei competes in the men's rings final of the artistic gymnastics at the 2008 Olympic Games.

▲ Russia's Daria Kondakova performs a routine with the ribbon during the 2009 Rhythmic Gymnastics World Championships. Daria along with three other gymnasts from Russia won the team competition.

The event includes separate competitions for individual apparatus, all-around individual competitions and team competitions. There are also world championships for trampolining and rhythmic gymnastics.

Scoring for artistic gymnastics events used to be out of ten. Nadia Comaneci is famous for being the first gymnast to receive a perfect ten score. She achieved this at the 1976 Olympics on the uneven bars.

Since 2006, the marking system has changed. Now, a gymnast's score is in two parts. These judge how difficult the routine was and how well it was performed. Top scores at many competitions are between 15 and 17.

# Where next?

These websites and books will help you find out more about gymnastics.

http://www.british-gymnastics.org/site/
The homepage of British Gymnastics, the organisation that runs gymnastics in Britain.

http://www.usa-gymnastics.org/
The official website of the organisation that runs gymnastics in America is full of biographies and pictures of leading gymnasts in action.

http://www.gymnasticsrevolution.com/GymInteractive-Index.htm
A great website with photos, diagrams and written tips of lots of individual moves from handstands in floor exercises to handsprings when vaulting.

http://gymnasticszone.com/ToughGymnast.htm
Read the full, amazing story of Shun Fujimoto's brave performances at the 1976 Olympics at this website packed with gymnastics news and features.

http://www.youtube.com/gymnstands2
This YouTube channel contains lots of short videos of top gymnasts performing routines.

http://www.brentwoodtc.org/trampolining.htm
Brentwood Trampolining Club's website contains lots of information on common trampolining moves.

## Books

*How To Improve At Gymnastics – Heather Brown (Crabtree, 2009).*
A great, simple guide to common moves used in gymnastics routines.

*Know The Game: Gymnastics – British Gymnastics and Brian Stocks (A&C Black, 2008).*
A detailed look at gymnastics rules, moves, equipment and skills.

# Gymnastics words

**apparatus** any of the pieces of equipment used in a gymnastics competition, such as the balance beam or pommel horse

**arabesque** a body position in which one leg is raised and stretched out behind the gymnast

**artistic gymnastics** gymnastics performed on pieces of apparatus such as the floor, the vaulting table and the bars

**balance** the ability to hold a position without toppling or losing control

**chalk box** a container holding powdered chalk into which gymnasts can dip their hands to help get a better grip on the apparatus

**coordination** organising your brain, muscles and body parts to work together well

**elite** top performers in a sport

**flexibility** the physical ability to perform a wide range of movements

**rhythmic gymnastics** routines mainly done by girls, in which gymnasts perform to music using a ball, hoop, rope, ribbon or clubs

**straddle** a body position in which the body faces forward and the legs are spread far apart to the side

**synchronised** working together at the same time

**tuck** a body position in which the knees and hips are bent and brought into the chest

**vault** an artistic gymnastics event in which gymnasts run down a runway, jump off a springboard and spring off a vaulting table

# Index